First Facts™

Positively Pets

Caring for Your Cat

by Erika L. Shores

Consultant:
Jennifer Zablotny, DVM
Member, American Veterinary Medical Association

Capstone
press®
Mankato, Minnesota

First Facts is published by Capstone Press,
151 Good Counsel Drive, P.O. Box 669, Mankato, Minnesota 56002.
www.capstonepress.com

Library of Congress Cataloging-in-Publication Data
Shores, Erika L., 1976–
    Caring for your cat / Erika L. Shores.
    p. cm.—(First facts. Positively pets)
    Summary: "Describes caring for a cat, including supplies needed, feeding, cleaning,
health, safety, and aging"—Provided by publisher.
    Includes bibliographical references and index.
    ISBN-13: 978-0-7368-6384-1 (hardcover)
    ISBN-10: 0-7368-6384-2 (hardcover)
    1. Cats—Juvenile literature. I. Title. II. Series
SF445.7.S55 2007
636.8—dc22   2005035851

Editorial Credits

Becky Viaene, editor; Bobbi J. Wyss, designer; Kim Brown, illustrator; Kelly Garvin,
    photo researcher/photo editor

Photo Credits

Ardea/Ardea London, 16–17; Ardea/Jean Michel Labat, 18; Ardea/John Daniels, 7; Capstone
Press/Karon Dubke, 5, 6, 12, 13; Corbis, cover; Corbis/Jim Craigmyle, 15; Lynn M. Stone, 20;
Norvia Behling, 10–11; Photodisc, 21; SuperStock/age fotostock, 8

Capstone Press thanks the Kind Veterinary Clinic, Saint Peter, Minnesota, for their assistance
with this book.

The author dedicates this book to her parents, Richard and Betty Mikkelson of Faribault,
Minnesota.

1 2 3 4 5 6 11 10 09 08 07 06

Table of Contents

So You Want to Own a Cat?

You love the way they purr and **pounce**. You've heard about cats at **shelters** needing homes. Or maybe your neighbor is giving away kittens. You want a cat, but are you ready for the responsibility?

It's important to learn how to care for a cat before you get one. It's the best way to help your cat live a long life.

I'm the most popular pet in the United States. Almost 78 million cats are kept as pets.

Supplies to Buy

You'll need to get supplies for your cat. It must have food, water, and a litter box filled with litter. You can also get a food dish, a water bowl, and a brush.

Scratching posts and toys keep cats from getting bored. Cats who don't have scratching posts are more likely to dig their sharp claws into the furniture.

Your Cat at Home

Where's the new cat? Look under your bed. Cats are often scared in new places. Help your pet get used to your house. Keep it in one room for a few days. In time, the cat will want to explore your home.

I love to play, especially with feathers and toy mice. But strings, ribbons, and rubber bands are dangerous for me. I could swallow them and get sick or even die.

Feeding Your Cat

Meow! Your cat may be saying, "I'm hungry!" Give your cat fresh water and food every day. Most kittens eat three meals a day, but grown cats eat two. Cat food bags tell you how much food to give your cat.

I might think I like milk, but really it upsets my stomach. Fresh water is the best thing for me to drink.

Cleaning

While **grooming** its fur, a cat swallows
some hair. The hair forms hairballs in
the stomach. Brushing your cat removes
loose hair and prevents hairballs.

Cats use a litter box only if it is clean. Scoop out soiled litter from the box every day. Once a week, remove the old litter. Put in fresh litter.

A Visit to the Vet

   Veterinarians are doctors who help keep animals healthy. You should take your adult cat to a vet once a year for shots and a checkup.

   At about 6 months old, cats can be **spayed** or **neutered** to prevent unwanted kittens. Fewer unwanted kittens means less-crowded shelters.

Your Cat with Other Pets

Have you heard the saying about fighting like cats and dogs? Cats do get along with other pets, but it may take time. Slowly introduce other pets to your new cat.

Never leave birds or other small pets alone with a cat. By **instinct**, cats hunt smaller animals.

Your Cat's Life

You and your cat should become longtime friends. Cats can live for 12 to 20 years. Good food, exercise, and checkups help keep cats healthy.

As your cat ages, it will sleep more and eat less. Your vet can tell you how to care for an aging cat. Make the most of the years you have together.

Wild Relatives!

When a cat pounces on a spider, she's acting like her wild relatives. Lions, tigers, and leopards are wild cats that are related to your pet. Just like your cat, wild cats sleep most of the day. They are active in the evening and early morning when they hunt.

Decode Your Cat's Behavior

- Cats curl their tails around you to greet you. They raise their tails when they're excited or curious. But quick, large tail movements mean they are annoyed.

- Cats often purr to show they're comfortable. Some also purr when they're in pain or afraid.

- Cats hiss when they are angry and meow when they are hungry, need help, or want attention.

- When cats arch their backs and their fur stands up, they are scared or angry. Stay back!

- Cats rub against your legs and roll on their backs when they are content.

Glossary

groom (GROOM)—to clean; cats groom themselves by licking their fur.

instinct (IN-stingkt)—behavior that is natural rather than learned

neuter (NOO-tur)—to operate on a male animal so it is unable to produce young

pounce (POUNSS)—to jump on something suddenly and grab it

shelter (SHEL-tur)—a place where homeless animals can stay

spay (SPAY)—to operate on a female animal so it is unable to produce young

veterinarian (vet-ur-uh-NER-ee-uhn)—a doctor who treats sick or injured animals; veterinarians also help animals stay healthy.

Read More

Blackaby, Susan. *A Cat for You: Caring for Your Cat.* Pet Care. Minneapolis: Picture Window Books, 2003.

Ganeri, Anita. *Cats.* A Pet's Life. Chicago: Heinemann, 2003.

Hibbert, Clare. *Cat.* Looking after Your Pet. North Mankato, Minn.: Smart Apple Media, 2005.

Internet Sites

FactHound offers a safe, fun way to find Internet sites related to this book. All of the sites on FactHound have been researched by our staff.

Here's how:

1. Visit *www.facthound.com*

2. Choose your grade level.

3. Type in this book ID **0736863842** for age-appropriate sites. You may also browse subjects by clicking on letters, or by clicking on pictures and words.

4. Click on the **Fetch It** button.

FactHound will fetch the best sites for you!

Index